The Way of the Cross

The Way *of the* Cross

ARCHBISHOP GEORG GÄNSWEIN

Translated by Michael J. Miller

SOPHIA INSTITUTE PRESS
MANCHESTER, NH

Sophia Institute Press
Box 5284, Manchester, NH 03108
1-800-888-9344

www.SophiaInstitute.com

Sophia Institute Press® is a registered trademark of Sophia Institute.

Library of Congress Control Number: 2020935177

ISBN: 978-1-64413-308-8
First printing

Contents

Foreword: Baroness Nina Sophie Heereman von Zuydtwyck 3

First Station: Jesus is condemned to death 9

Second Station: Jesus shoulders the Cross 13

Third Station: Jesus falls the first time under the Cross 17

Fourth Station: Jesus meets His Mother 21

Fifth Station: Simon helps Jesus to carry the Cross 25

Sixth Station: Veronica wipes the face of Jesus 29

Seventh Station: Jesus falls the second time under the Cross 33

Eighth Station: Jesus meets the weeping women 37

Ninth Station: Jesus falls the third time under the cross 41

Tenth Station: Jesus is stripped of His garments 45

Eleventh Station: Jesus is nailed to the Cross 49

Twelfth Station: Jesus dies on the Cross 53

Thirteenth Station: Jesus is taken down from the Cross 57

Fourteenth Station: Jesus is laid in the tomb 61

Appendix: Prayers 65

Illustrations

Frescos by Martin Feuerstein (1856–1931)

Jesus Condemned to Die, 1st Station of the Cross 11

Jesus Shoulders the Cross, 2nd Station of the Cross 15

Jesus Falls the First Time, 3rd Station of the Cross 19

Jesus Meets His Mother, 4th Station of the Cross 23

Simon of Cyrene Helps Carry the Cross, 5th Station of the Cross 27

Veronica Wipes the Face of Jesus, 6th Station of the Cross 31

Jesus Falls the Second Time, 7th Station of the Cross 35

Jesus Meets the Weeping Women, 8th Station of the Cross 39

Jesus Falls the Third Time, 9th Station of the Cross 43

Jesus Stripped of His Garments, 10th Station of the Cross 47

Jesus Nailed to the Cross, 11th Station of the Cross 51

Jesus Dies on the Cross, 12th Station of the Cross 55

Jesus Taken Down from the Cross, 13th Station of the Cross 59

The Deposition of the Body, 14th Station of the Cross 63

These beautiful frescos, which were painted in 1898 in the Saint Anna Church, in Munich, Germany, have since been painted over. Color images nave been preserved of only thirteen of the fourteen Stations. We have added some color to the surviving monocrome image of the 6th Station for these meditations.

Stations of the Cross

On Fridays during Lent, Catholics traditionally reflect upon the Stations of the Cross, fourteen memorable events that occurred from the moment Christ was condemned to death to His placement in the tomb. Catholics reflect upon the Stations of the Cross as a way of spiritually walking and praying with Christ as He journeys to the place of His Crucifixion. The Stations are usually placed around the inside perimeter of a church. It is customary to genuflect at each Station, meditate upon the scene, and say, "We adore You, O Christ, and we bless You; because by Your holy Cross, You have redeemed the world."

During the Crusades (1095–1270), pilgrims visited the Holy Land to walk the path taken by Christ. For Catholics who did not have the opportunity to visit the Holy Land, churches began erecting wooden images of the Stations outside, and eventually, images of the Stations were placed inside churches. The Franciscan priest St. Leonard of Port Maurice promoted the Stations of the Cross in the 1700s and erected hundreds of Stations throughout Italy.

—Helen Hoffner, *Catholic Traditions and Treasures*
(Manchester, NH: Sophia Institute Press, 2018), 33-34

Jesus on His final path through the Holy Land

Accompanying a dying person on his final path is one of the noblest works of Christian mercy. Never is a human being so lonely as in the final hours of his life, since he must walk through the gate of death alone. Although we cannot spare one another this path through the darkness, we can nevertheless accompany the dying person lovingly up to the gate of death, in the firm hope that the merciful Lord will welcome him into the hereafter.

With Jesus it was different. For Him the path led not only to His cruel death on the Cross, which is bad enough, but into the darkest cavities of the underworld. Not only that: on His final path, He was abandoned by everyone, even His closest confidants. Only His Mother, a few women who had followed Him from Galilee, and John—the only one of the twelve apostles—stood beneath Him in His final hours and watched His eyes glaze over. The Son of God felt abandoned even by His Father, having taken upon Himself vicariously the unfathomable abandonment of the sinner, in order to admit us all again into communion with the Father through His death. No one, not even the worst sinner, will ever have to endure again that kind of abandonment in the hour of his death.

Have you ever wondered where you would have been in those hours? Don't we all wish secretly that we had the courage of those women, whose love had led them there beneath the Cross, or the love of John, who was faithful to the Friend "whom he loved" even into the jet-black night of death?

Well, it is not true that we can no longer perform this loving service for the Lord. On the contrary, in prayerful remembrance of His Passion, we can go beyond the boundaries of space and time and, by dint of our faith, walk beside Jesus on His final path through the Holy Land, consoling Him with our love. In this way, we can be like Mary: a pious tradition in Jerusalem relates to this day that after the Ascension of the Lord she returned every day to the stations of His Passion in order to meditate lovingly in her heart on what He suffered for us and on the great love with which He loved us.

Following this example of the Mother of God, the Church developed the practice of praying the Way of the Cross, first in Jerusalem, and later throughout the world. For centuries, especially on Fridays, Christians have followed in spirit their Lord's Way of the Cross. By doing so, they seek to be close to Him and, at the same time, to draw from their meditation on His Passion the strength to carry their own crosses after Him. The difficulty that almost all of us encounter in doing so, however, is that, unlike Mary, we cannot draw on the memory of what we ourselves have experienced. Yes, it is extraordinarily difficult for us to imagine vividly the events of that day and the circumstances of the Crucifixion, which are so foreign to us. For this reason, there have always been guides to meditation in the form of Way of the Cross devotions.

In recent decades, certainly, it has become difficult to find meditations that really help us to encounter Jesus on His Way of the Cross. The great majority of them set before our eyes the misery of today's world, which the Lord did make His own, but since it bears His countenance only indirectly, it cannot show us "what great love the Father had given us" in His suffering Son (see 1 John 3:1). A well-done Way of the Cross, in contrast, enables us to see His original and uniquely beautiful countenance and carries the devotee off to Jerusalem, right up to Mount Zion and the hill of Golgotha, where he finds himself in the midst of the Jewish people and becomes an eyewitness.

Such a Way of the Cross is given to us now by Archbishop Georg Gänswein in this precious booklet. In response to a request by the almost hundred-year-old artist Auguste Maria Karoline Moede Jansens, who created the vignettes for this Way of the Cross, the faithful secretary of Pope Benedict XVI now depicts here "the final path of Jesus through the Holy Land" so as to give the impression that we are really there. Like Mel Gibson in his *Passion of the Christ*, the former prefect of the Papal Household in Rome depicts these two-thousand-year-old events so vividly that the prayerful reader will feel as if he has been taken back to Jerusalem in the year of the Lord 33 and, at the sight of Jesus' suffering, will be profoundly moved by God's love.

From the living encounter with Love-who-became-man that is made possible in this way, the prayerful reader will receive in a wonderful way the strength to help Jesus, in His suffering sisters and brothers, to carry the cross, the courage not to deny Him when he himself is persecuted, ridiculed, and slandered for His Name's sake, and the willingness to accept his own cross, so as to persevere faithfully, even unto the end, in that love which is stronger than death.

Baroness Nina Sophie Heereman von Zuydtwyck
Jerusalem, January 7, 2020

5

The
Stations
of the
Cross

I. STATION

Jesus is condemned to death

V: We adore You, O Christ, and we bless You,
R: Because by Your holy Cross You have redeemed the world.

> Pilate, wishing to satisfy the crowd,
> released for them Barabbas;
> and having scourged Jesus,
> he delivered Him to be crucified.
> Mark 15:15

I

Jesus is condemned to death

During the night, all of Jesus' apostles abandoned Him. His closest friends had fallen asleep as the fear of death overcame them. He was betrayed, though, with a kiss, the most intimate sign of love. He was condemned to death that same night by the tribunal of the high priest, with a judgment that had long since been passed. He was also beaten then, right before the eyes of the judge. Now, though, He stands before the highest secular authority of Jerusalem, the representative of the mighty emperor in Rome. In this trial He has no advocate. Nevertheless Pilate hesitates for a long time with the sentence, because he can find no guilt in Him.

"What is truth?" the governor asks Him, when the Truth is standing before him in the flesh. Then he has Him scourged, crowned by his soldiers with a cap of thorns and mocked, and he himself speaks a truth until the end of days when he presents Him to the furious crowd that is demanding His death.

"Behold the man," he exclaims as he shows them the Man of all men, the "Son of man," the first and last Image of all the images of God. Then he has a servant bring a bowl of water and washes his hands in innocence. Seconds before that, he delivers the accused man over to his persecutors with the words: "Take Him and crucify Him."

R: Our Father..., Hail Mary..., Glory be...

R: At the Cross, her station keeping,
   stood the mournful Mother weeping,
   close to Jesus to the last.

V: Crucified and risen Lord Jesus Christ,

R: Have mercy on us and on the whole world.

II. STATION

Jesus shoulders the Cross

V: We adore You, O Christ, and we bless You,
R: Because by Your holy Cross You have redeemed the world.

> Jesus went out, bearing His own cross,
> to the place called the place of a skull,
> which is called in Hebrew Golgotha.
> John 19:17

II

Jesus shoulders the Cross

At the top of the staircase leading to Pilate's palace, Jesus appears, covered with blood, wearing a blood-red soldier's cloak. Staggering, He totters down the steps. Thorns as long as a thumb have gotten under His scalp, encircling His field of vision. Behold the man! His blood drips onto the white marble. Here, at the beginning of the Way of the Cross, He seems about to fall already, in the middle of the staircase. A legionary holds up in front of Him the guilty verdict on a board: "Jesus of Nazareth, King of the Jews."

Below in the courtyard, He meets two other condemned men who are also "going to the cross," as the Romans call this path: brawny, unscrupulous highwaymen guilty of murder, who now are losing their own lives. They were not scourged; they were not mocked with a crown of thorns. Jesus is now lined up between these murderers.

He seems about to collapse when the legionaries lift the heavy wooden Cross onto His shoulders. He totters again and staggers out of the palace courtyard onto the street, to His final path through the Holy Land.

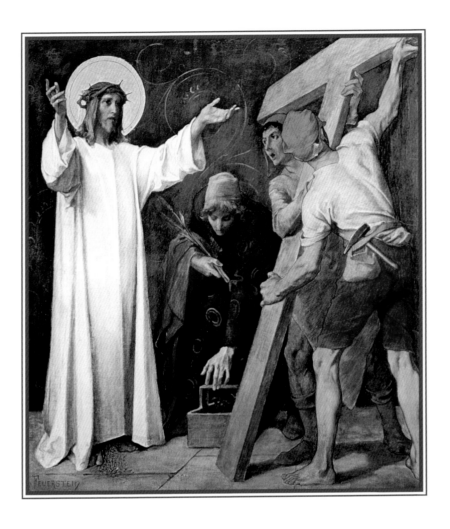

R: Our Father..., Hail Mary..., Glory be...

R: Through her heart, His sorrow sharing,
   all His bitter anguish bearing,
   now at length the sword had passed.

V: Crucified and risen Lord Jesus Christ,

R: Have mercy on us and on the whole world.

III. STATION

Jesus falls the first time under the Cross

V: We adore You, O Christ, and we bless You,
R: Because by Your holy Cross You have redeemed the world.

> Unless a grain of wheat falls into the earth and dies,
> it remains alone;
> but if it dies, it bears much fruit.
> John 12:24

Jesus stumbles through the crowded bazaar. A throng of people prevents Him from going forward. Tomorrow is Pascha, Jerusalem's most solemn feast. It is the feast of the "Passover of the Lord," which the Lord was not to experience again. The verdict against Him was issued on this eve of the feast, on the "Day of Preparation." Now everyone in the city is in a hurry. All Jerusalem is up and about, before the feast begins right at dusk—a feast that no one celebrates alone here. Everyone in the crowd through which Jesus drags the wood of His Cross is loaded down with last-minute purchases and provisions. A squad of executioners from the Roman Legion with clubs and whips brutally clears a way for Him through the festive crowd.

Suddenly He falls. Did He stumble on a projecting stone? On an outstretched foot? Did someone trip Him up? Hard to say. Wickedness does not diminish in the face of the Holy One, but rather increases. The executioners' blows continue to rain down on Him.

R: Our Father..., Hail Mary..., Glory be...

R: Oh, how sad and sore distressèd,
was that Mother highly blessèd,
of the sole-begotten One!

V: Crucified and risen Lord Jesus Christ,

R: Have mercy on us and on the whole world.

IV. STATION

Jesus meets His Mother

V: We adore You, O Christ, and we bless You,
R: Because by Your holy Cross You have redeemed the world.

Simeon said to Mary His Mother:
"Behold, this child is set
for the fall and rising of many in Israel
and for a sign that is spoken against;
and a sword will pierce through your own soul also."
Luke 2:34-35

Jesus meets His Mother

Then suddenly Mary, Jesus' Mother looks at Him from the crowd. Through the tumult, she has made her way to the front to meet Him. She has followed Him since the days in Galilee. Did she wait for Him behind an archway? "His hour has not yet come," she knew three years ago in Cana. Now she is there again and knows that His final hour has struck, but she only watches, in unspeakable sorrow. Her only Son, the One and All of the whole world: He, too, is silent and watches—only looks at her.

Blood runs down His face from the wounds of the thorns as their glances meet. Two seconds? Three seconds? An eternity. Mary falls to the ground, stretches out her arms toward Him. Then the legionaries, with their clubs and their rough shouts, drive her aside into the crowd of bazaar-goers, among the bystanders watching the spectacle of the execution.

R: Our Father..., Hail Mary..., Glory be...

R: Christ above in torment hangs;
   she beneath beholds the pangs
   of her dying, glorious Son!

V: Crucified and risen Lord Jesus Christ,

R: Have mercy on us and on the whole world.

V. STATION

Simon helps Jesus to carry the Cross

V: We adore You, O Christ, and we bless You,
R: Because by Your holy Cross You have redeemed the world.

> They compelled a passer-by,
> Simon of Cyrene, who was coming in from the country,
> the father of Alexander and Rufus,
> to carry His cross.
> Mark 15:21

The streets through which the squad drives Jesus on ahead are so narrow. At the next corner, Jesus totters, apparently about to collapse, as though He could never complete His final path alive, too weak for the Crucifixion.

On the spot, the centurion of the execution squad gives the order, and a man from the crowd, on the way from the field to the market with his sons, is seized and forced to help the criminal, who has lost a great deal of blood, to carry His heavy load. Arbitrariness is the law of the occupying forces.

Yet the Cross is heavy even for two men, especially in the tumult of the crowd and on the rough pavement of the bazaar. Carrying together has to be learned for these two men who now stagger together under the heavy weight of the lethal wood toward the hill of death.

R: Our Father..., Hail Mary..., Glory be...

R: Is there one who would not weep,
'whelmed in miseries so deep,
Christ's dear Mother to behold?

V: Crucified and risen Lord Jesus Christ,

R: Have mercy on us and on the whole world.

VI. STATION

Veronica wipes the face of Jesus

V: We adore You, O Christ, and we bless You,
R: Because by Your holy Cross You have redeemed the world.

> He had no form or comeliness
> that we should look at Him,
> and no beauty that we should desire Him.
> He was despised and rejected by men...
> as one from whom men hide their faces.
> Isa. 53:2-3

Suddenly a woman rushes toward Jesus—not His Mother, not Mary Magdalene. None of the apostles and companions from Galilee is around Jesus on His final path, except John, who earlier was standing beside His Mother. The brutality of the soldiers does not frighten this woman away. With a cloth in her hand, she wipes the blood from Jesus' beautiful face, contorted by pain, and presses the cloth with the imprint of the bloody streams to her heart like a treasure as she disappears again into the crowd: O bleeding Head, so wounded. Flies buzz around Him.

R: Our Father..., Hail Mary..., Glory be...

R: Can the human heart refrain
 from partaking in her pain,
 in that Mother's pain untold?

V: Crucified and risen Lord Jesus Christ,

R: Have mercy on us and on the whole world.

VII. STATION

Jesus falls the second time under the Cross

V: We adore You, O Christ, and we bless You,
R: Because by Your holy Cross You have redeemed the world.

Jesus said to His disciples:
"My soul is very sorrowful, even to death."
And going a little farther,
He fell on the ground and prayed
that, if it were possible,
the hour might pass from Him.
Mark 14:34–35

The way from Pilate's palace to the Place of the Skull, which in Hebrew is called Golgotha, is scarcely one mile long. Yet it seems endless, and now Jesus has fallen to the ground under the weight of the Cross for the second time already. First onto His knees and then flat on His face on the stones. His nose is bleeding. Soldiers haul Him up, set Him on His feet, and drive Him onward.

R: Our Father..., Hail Mary..., Glory be...

R: Bruised, derided, cursed, defiled,
   she beheld her tender Child,
   all with bloody scourges rent.

V: Crucified and risen Lord Jesus Christ,

R: Have mercy on us and on the whole world.

VIII. STATION

Jesus meets the weeping women

V: We adore You, O Christ, and we bless You,
R: Because by Your holy Cross You have redeemed the world.

> There followed Him a great multitude of the people,
> and of women who bewailed and lamented Him.
> But Jesus turning to them said,
> "Daughters of Jerusalem, do not weep for me,
> but weep for yourselves and for your children."
> Luke 23:27-28

All the noise of the streets and the marketplace is suddenly drowned out by the lament of women with their children. The women are acquainted with the condemned Man as an eloquent Teacher and Savior. Now they wail, as has been the custom from time immemorial in the Middle East when a dead man is to be mourned. But Jesus is still alive, and here He breaks His silence for the first time since setting out from Pilate's courtyard. He turns to the wailing women and says: "Daughters of Jerusalem, do not weep for me, but weep for yourselves and for your children. For behold, the days are coming when they will say, 'Blessed are the barren, and the wombs that never bore, and the breasts that never nursed.' Then they will begin to say to the mountains, 'Fall on us'; and to the hills, 'Cover us.' For if they do this when the wood is green, what will happen when it is dry?" (Luke 23:28–31). He gasps. His voice almost fails. We understand Him very little or not at all, and nevertheless through all the generations the words are imprinted on our souls like a seal: "Weep for yourselves and for your children!"

R: Our Father..., Hail Mary..., Glory be...
R: For the sins of His own nation
   saw Him hang in desolation
   till His spirit forth He sent.
V: Crucified and risen Lord Jesus Christ,
R: Have mercy on us and on the whole world.

IX. STATION

Jesus falls the third time under the Cross

V: We adore You, O Christ, and we bless You,
R: Because by Your holy Cross You have redeemed the world.

Come to me,
all who labor and are heavy laden,
and I will give you rest.
Take my yoke upon you,
and learn from me;
for I am gentle and lowly in heart,
and you will find rest for your souls.
For my yoke is easy,
and my burden is light.
Matt. 11:28–30

At the Garden Gate, Jesus' final path brings Him at last out of the narrow city and its commercial agitation to Golgotha, outside the city wall. This is the rock for Jerusalem's executions, the hilltop gallows for the capital. It is a crude chunk of rock in an abandoned quarry, a bit taller than the battlements of the wall, perhaps a stone's throw from the Garden Gate. Right now sheep and lambs from the fields are being driven through the Garden Gate into the city as sacrificial animals for the Temple and for the many festive meals. Here Jesus goes out into the open in deafening confusion. The air is filled with dust and the bleating of lambs as Jesus, in the midst of them, falls once again under the Cross, and the man from Cyrene, whom the soldiers forced to help carry it, cannot prevent it. The Lord lies stretched out on the ground. His bare collarbone gleams pale beneath the large wound that the rough wood of the Cross has gouged in His left shoulder. It must cause Him more pain than all the other wounds together, yet He no longer opens His mouth.

The sun grows dark. Desert wind covers the sky with its clouds of dust. One last time, Jesus is yanked up and driven onward, toward the quarry, through a garden, and up the rock hill.

R: Our Father..., Hail Mary..., Glory be...

R: O sweet Mother! font of love,
   touch my spirit from above,
   make my heart with yours accord.

V: Crucified and risen Lord Jesus Christ,

R: Have mercy on us and on the whole world.

X. STATION

Jesus is stripped of His garments

V: We adore You, O Christ, and we bless You,
R: Because by Your holy Cross You have redeemed the world.

> They divided His garments among them,
> casting lots for them,
> to decide what each should take.
> Mark 15:24

U p here Jesus is finally al-
lowed to let the Cross
fall from His shoulder.
But not only the Cross is taken
from Him. He is also stripped of
His garments, until the scourged
man stands bloody in front of
the soldiers and the onlookers of
Jerusalem.

R: Our Father..., Hail Mary..., Glory be...
R: Make me feel as you have felt,
   make my soul to glow and melt
   with the love of Christ, my Lord.
V: Crucified and risen Lord Jesus Christ,
R: Have mercy on us and on the whole world.

XI. STATION

Jesus is nailed to the Cross

V: We adore You, O Christ, and we bless You,
R: Because by Your holy Cross You have redeemed the world.

It was the third hour when they crucified Him.
And the inscription of the charge against Him read:
"The King of the Jews."
And with Him they crucified two robbers,
one on His right and one on His left.
Mark 15:25-27

So the soldiers nail Jesus to the Cross on the ground, with big, rough nails, which they drive through His wrists separately and through His feet, placed one over the other on a little block of wood fastened to the Cross. That way, He can push off from it to draw breath and postpone imminent death by suffocation when the Cross stands vertical in the ground. He has turned down the drugged potion. He knows that He will die now and wants to do it with His mind clear.

R: Our Father..., Hail Mary..., Glory be...

R: Holy Mother, pierce me through,
   in my heart each wound renew
   of my Savior crucified.

V: Crucified and risen Lord Jesus Christ,

R: Have mercy on us and on the whole world.

XII. STATION

Jesus dies on the Cross

V: We adore You, O Christ, and we bless You,
R: Because by Your holy Cross You have redeemed the world.

When the sixth hour had come,
there was darkness over the whole land
until the ninth hour.
And at the ninth hour
Jesus cried with a loud voice,
"Eloi, Eloi, lama sabachthani?" which means,
"My God, My God, why have you forsaken Me?"...
And a bystander ran and, filling a sponge full of vinegar,
put it on a reed and gave it to Him to drink....
And Jesus uttered a loud cry,
and breathed His last....
When the centurion, who stood facing Jesus,
saw that He thus breathed His last, he said,
"Truly this man was the Son of God!"
Mark 15:33–39

Jesus dies on the Cross

Along with the Cross of Jesus, the crosses of the two robbers and murderers are set up, apocalyptically choreographed, one to His right, the other to His left. But of the three men, only He wears a crown; only He has hanging over His head the verdict that was carried before Him earlier through the streets: "King of the Jews!" Beyond the city wall He can look over to the Mount of Olives in the East and to the Temple on the Temple Mount, to "His Father's house," as He called this place of worship since His childhood, where now to the sound of rams' horns the lambs are being slain for the Passover feast.

The bystanders who followed the criminals earlier through the bazaar jeer at Him, not at the two criminals on His right and His left. They wag their heads and exclaim: "You want to tear down the Temple and in three days build it up again? Do it, then!" Others mockingly kneel down. The twisted worm on the cross can scarcely see them, because He can no longer wipe the blood from His eyes. He can do nothing at all now. His Mother, overwhelmed with sorrow below Him, with John, His beloved disciple, and Mary Magdalene—all have dissolved into

tears. All the other apostles, who wanted to sit beside Him in heaven, have fled. Far and wide Peter is not to be seen. Instead, the high priests, the scribes, and the elders have come outside the city. They want to see with their own eyes that He finally dies. They want to be there as witnesses to vouch for the fact that this imaginary "King of Israel" cannot climb down from the Cross like a magician. Meanwhile it has become as black as night in broad daylight. The sun is darkened.

Jesus can scarcely draw breath, but haltingly begins to stammer Psalm 22 and to call: "My God, my God, why have You forsaken me? Why are You so far from helping me, from the words of my groaning?... But I am a worm, and no man, scorned by men, and despised by the people." Then He cries out loudly once more and dies.

The psalm ends with: "Dominion belongs to the LORD, and He rules over the nations. Yes, to Him shall all the proud of the earth bow down.... To Him my soul shall live" (see Ps. 21[22]:31, Douay-Rheims). But Jesus prays these words to their conclusion only in Paradise, where He also meets again the poor wretch, the criminal on His right side, to whom He promised it before drawing His last breath.

R: Our Father..., Hail Mary..., Glory be...
R: Let me share with you His pain,
   Who for all our sins was slain,
   Who for me in torments died.
V: Crucified and risen Lord Jesus Christ,
R: Have mercy on us and on the whole world.

XIII. <small>STATION</small>

Jesus is taken down from the Cross

V: We adore You, O Christ, and we bless You,
R: Because by Your holy Cross You have redeemed the world.

> Standing by the cross of Jesus were His Mother,
> and His Mother's sister, Mary the wife of Clopas,
> and Mary Magdalene....
> But when the soldiers came to Jesus
> and saw that He was already dead,...
> one of the soldiers pierced His side with a spear,
> and at once there came out blood and water....
> After this Joseph of Arimathea...
> asked Pilate that he might take away the body of Jesus.
> John 19:25, 33–34, 38

XIII. Jesus is taken down from the Cross

An officer rams his spear with full force into Jesus' side in order to certify His death officially, as it were. Blood and water gush from the wound and down from the Cross like a spring onto the ground, while other legionaries to the left and right of him break the legs of the criminals, so that they can no longer support themselves to catch their breath and finally will suffocate quickly before the feast begins. Only Jesus' bones remain intact. Then an earthquake shakes Jerusalem and splits Golgotha from top to bottom, and the Roman centurion cries out in shock: "Truly, this was the Son of God!" (Matt. 27:54).

Haste is called for now. Before the evening star appears in the sky, the Place of the Skull must be cleared of all traces of the execution. It is anything but simple, though, to free the lifeless Lord from the nails fastening Him to the Cross. The Romans don't help. Skilled personnel are not there. And the apostles have fled, except John, the youngest. Joseph of Arimathea, though, a secret disciple of Jesus and a member of the high council, has obtained from Pilate permission to bury the body in a new tomb that he had hewn for himself in a rock not far from Golgotha, and he quickly purchased a large, very fine, clean linen cloth for the burial. So he and Nicodemus, another councilor, together with John, remove the big nails from the wounds and the wood. Heavy tongs are necessary for that. No sooner is the right arm free than Jesus' body sags, and blood and water gush upward from His lung and out of His mouth. John presses a linen cloth to the Lord's face to keep the blood from falling on the ground. The desert wind is still darkening the pale sky. In this twilight, the three men lay the lifeless body of the Son on the knees of the weary Mother, who had mourned His death at the foot of the Cross, together with Mary Magdalene and "Mary, the mother of Joses." Only two hours away to the south by foot is Bethlehem, where she laid Him on her lap for the first time. Then it was with sighs; now it is in voiceless sorrow.

R: Our Father..., Hail Mary..., Glory be...

R: Let me mingle tears with thee,
   mourning Him who mourned for me,
   all the days that I may live.

V: Crucified and risen Lord Jesus Christ,

R: Have mercy on us and on the whole world.

XIV. STATION

Jesus is laid in the tomb

V: We adore You, O Christ, and we bless You,
R: Because by Your holy Cross You have redeemed the world.

When Pilate learned from the centurion
that Jesus was dead,
he granted the body to Joseph.
And he bought a linen shroud,
and taking Him down, wrapped Him in the linen shroud
and laid Him in a tomb
which had been hewn out of the rock;
and he rolled a stone against the door of the tomb.
Mary Magdalene and Mary the mother of Joses
saw where He was laid.
Mark 15:45–47

XIV. Jesus is laid in the tomb

Nicodemus cleans and anoints the wounds diligently with myrrh and aloe. He has purchased an extravagant amount for this purpose, regardless of the cost. Then the men wrap Jesus' body in Joseph's expensive linen shroud and carry the body down the hill to the new tomb in the garden, where they lay it carefully on the rock bench in the second chamber to the right. Caution is called for at every step. Only the women followed them. Then Joseph rolls the stone to close off the burial chamber. The Lord was killed like a criminal. But now He rests like a king in His tomb. A heavenly fragrance fills the cave and makes its way past the heavy stone into the open air in this garden beneath the Place of the Skull. Then the evening star, Venus, appears with its first gleam in the sky, and there is no end to the sounding of the rams' horns, as they proclaim from the Temple the feast of Israel's liberation from slavery, the beginning of the feast of Passover.

R: Our Father..., Hail Mary..., Glory be...

R: While my body here decays,
   may my soul Your goodness praise,
   safe in heaven eternally!

V: Crucified and risen Lord Jesus Christ,

R: Have mercy on us and on the whole world.

APPENDIX

Prayers

Prayers

The Sign of the Cross

In the name of the Father,
and of the Son,
and of the Holy Spirit.
Amen.

The Our Father

Our Father who art in Heaven,
hallowed be Thy name.
Thy kingdom come.
Thy will be done on earth,
as it is in Heaven.
Give us this day our daily bread,
and forgive us our trespasses,
as we forgive those who trespass against us,
and lead us not into temptation,
but deliver us from evil.
Amen.

The Hail Mary

Hail Mary, full of grace,
the Lord is with thee;
blessed art thou among women,
and blessed is the
fruit of thy womb, Jesus.
Holy Mary, Mother of God,
pray for us sinners,
now and at the hour of our death.
Amen.

The Glory Be

Glory be to the Father,
and to the Son,
and to the Holy Spirit;
as it was in the beginning,
is now, and ever shall be,
world without end.
Amen.

The Apostles' Creed

I believe in God, the Father almighty,
creator of Heaven and earth.
I believe in Jesus Christ,
His only Son, our Lord.
He was conceived
by the power of the Holy Spirit
and born of the Virgin Mary.
He suffered under Pontius Pilate,
was crucified, died, and was buried.
He descended into Hell.
On the third day He rose again.
He ascended into Heaven and
is seated at the right hand of the Father.
He will come again to judge
the living and the dead.
I believe in the Holy Spirit,
the holy Catholic Church,
the Communion of Saints,
the forgiveness of sins,
the resurrection of the body,
and the life everlasting.
Amen

Act of Contrition

O my God,
I am heartily sorry
for having offended Thee,
and I detest all my sins
because of Thy just punishments,
but most of all because they offend
Thee, my God, who art all good
and deserving of all my love.
I firmly resolve
with the help of Thy grace
to sin no more and
to avoid the near occasion of sin.
Amen.

About the Author

Archbishop Gänswein serves as Private Secretary for Pope Emeritus Benedict XVI and previously served as Prefect of the Papal Household for Pope Francis and as the chaplain to Pope John Paul II.

Sophia Institute

Sophia Institute is a nonprofit institution that seeks to nurture the spiritual, moral, and cultural life of souls and to spread the Gospel of Christ in conformity with the authentic teachings of the Roman Catholic Church.

Sophia Institute Press fulfills this mission by offering translations, reprints, and new publications that afford readers a rich source of the enduring wisdom of mankind. Sophia Institute also operates the popular online resource CatholicExchange.com. *Catholic Exchange* provides world news from a Catholic perspective as well as daily devotionals and articles that will help readers to grow in holiness and live a life consistent with the teachings of the Church.

In 2013, Sophia Institute launched Sophia Institute for Teachers to renew and rebuild Catholic culture through service to Catholic education. With the goal of nurturing the spiritual, moral, and cultural life of souls, and an abiding respect for the role and work of teachers, we strive to provide materials and programs that are at once enlightening to the mind and ennobling to the heart; faithful and complete, as well as useful and practical.

Sophia Institute gratefully recognizes the Solidarity Association for preserving and encouraging the growth of our apostolate over the course of many years. Without their generous and timely support, this book would not be in your hands.

www.SophiaInstitute.com
www.CatholicExchange.com
www.SophiaInstituteforTeachers.org

Sophia Institute Press® is a registered trademark of Sophia Institute. Sophia Institute is a tax-exempt institution as defined by the Internal Revenue Code, Section 501(c)(3). Tax I.D. 22-2548708.